PENCIL, PEN and BRUSH

by HARVEY WEISS

SCHOLASTIC BOOK SERVICES

NEW YORK • TORONTO • LONDON • AUCKLAND • SYDNEY • TOKYO

Acknowledgments

Thanks and acknowledgment are due the following museums, institutions, and individuals for their cooperation and help in the preparation of this book: The Metropolitan Museum of Art, New York; The Museum of Modern Art, New York; The Pierpont Morgan Library, New York; The Fogg Art Museum, Harvard University, Cambridge, Massachusetts; The Brooklyn Museum, Brooklyn, New York; The Royal Collection, Windsor Castle, England; Kraushaar Galleries, New York; Standard Oil Company (New Jersey); The French Embassy Press and Information Service, New York; The New York Zoological Society; May, Carla, Bill, John, Miriam. Special thanks are due Maurice Sendak and Joe Lasker, who very generously put their drawings and sketchbooks at the author's disposal.

Illustrations not otherwise credited are by the author.

Books by Harvey Weiss available in hardcover
editions from William R. Scott, Inc.:

CLAY, WOOD AND WIRE (sculpture)

PAPER, INK AND ROLLER (printmaking)

STICKS, SPOOLS AND FEATHERS (crafts)

CERAMICS: FROM CLAY TO KILN

PENCIL, PEN AND BRUSH

ISBN: 0-590-02229-6

Copyright © 1961 by Harvey Weiss. This edition is published by Scholastic Book Services, a division of Scholastic Magazines, Inc., by arrangement with Addison-Wesley Publishing Company, Inc.

21 20 19 18 17 16 15 14 13 12   0 1 2 3 4 5/8

Printed in the U.S.A.

REMBRANDT VAN RIJN

Contents

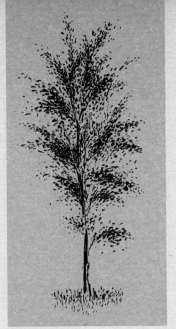

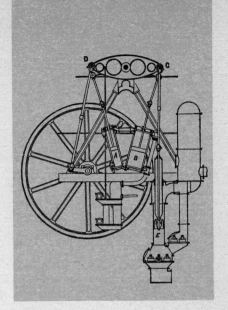

JOE LASKER   H. WEISS

Introduction

Drawing is a language without words. Often this language can tell you things faster and better than words. It is easier to *draw* a smile than to tell about it. A tree can be described more vividly in a drawing than by a series of words. And a diagram will explain, more clearly than any text, how a steam engine works.

In many professions today, drawing is an important means of explaining and clarifying ideas. The architect and the dress designer make drawings to show others what they have in mind and to demonstrate what has to be done. The sculptor makes drawings to explore and experiment with his ideas before proceeding to clay or stone. The potter, the airplane designer, the engineer, and in fact almost everybody concerned with building and creating uses drawing to explain and clarify ideas.

But drawing can be a very satisfying experience for its own sake. It doesn't have to have a purpose. It doesn't have to be serious or important. Drawing can be great fun, whether you keep your picture and frame it or just crumple it up and throw it away.

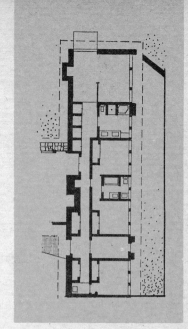

H. WEISS   LEONARDO DA VINCI

If you drew often enough, you would eventually discover, through trial and error, most of the techniques explained in this book. *Pencil, Pen and Brush* will speed up the learning process by allowing you to bypass some of the errors you might make if you drew without any help at all.

Each section of this book contains one or more "models." The models are photographs of people and animals and scenes. They are included so that you will have something from which to work. If you work from these photographs and follow the step-by-step directions and illustrations, you will be able to see exactly how a drawing develops. You will learn how to begin, what to try for, what to expect. After you've made one or two drawings from the photograph, you can go off on your own.

The book is divided into six sections. Each section concentrates on one or two particular aspects of drawing. Start at the beginning, and by the time you've worked through the book you will have an understanding of and some experience with the basic elements of drawing.

5

SAUL STEINBERG

JOE LASKER

MAURICE SENDAK

MAURICE SENDAK

Drawing Animals

What comes to mind when someone says "porcupine"? You probably think of prickly needles. Prickly needles sticking out in all directions — the special quality of porcupines.

Everything has a special quality, one which distinguishes its appearance or its actions. If you can learn to look for and recognize the special quality of the thing you are drawing, you will have gone a long way toward making a really successful picture.

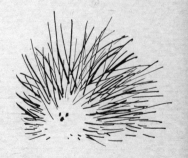

The artists who drew the animals on these pages all captured the special quality of their subjects. In the drawing of the bear, it is the rough, fuzzy coat. In the chicken, it is the fat, bulky look and all the wiggly feathers. Can you tell what special thing the artist found most interesting in his drawing of the lion?

How to Draw an Animal

Most live animals won't oblige by standing still while you draw them, so work at first from the photographs on the page opposite. The elephant's pose is an easy one to draw. Let's start with him.

MATERIALS: Get a pencil that will make a good dark line. You'll also need some sort of pencil sharpener. It's hard to draw with a short, blunted point. Almost any kind of paper will do, but make sure it is a good size—no smaller than nine by twelve inches. Find a sturdy and well-lighted table on which to work.

1. Before you start to draw, look carefully at the elephant. What is special about him? What makes him look different from a horse or a house or a giraffe? The special quality here is created by the large, heavy forms of the elephant's body—the simple, massive shape.

2. Think of the elephant as a collection of parts; this will help you to get everything in the correct proportion. The body is a big oval (an egg shape); the legs are like tree trunks; the head and ears are smaller ovals. Draw in these shapes, keeping them very light. This preliminary drawing is a "map" that shows you where everything is eventually going to be.

3. Now you can start putting in your heavier final lines. A pencil can make a great variety of lines — quick and sketchy, jiggly, heavy, any kind of line you like. Use a type of line that suits your elephant best.

4. When you have drawn the main shapes, tackle some of the smaller parts, such as the tail and tusks and trunk. Pick out only the most important details. Too many details will confuse the picture.

5. One distinctive feature of elephants is their skin. It has a rough texture; it is a tangle of wrinkles. "Texture" means the kind of surface that an object has. For example, silk has a smooth texture, sandpaper is rough, a wool rug is fuzzy. You can't make the paper itself smooth or rough or fuzzy. But you can *suggest* these qualities by the kind of pencil lines you make. See if you can get the texture of the elephant's skin in your drawing.

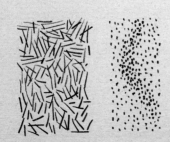   

6. Finally, when the elephant is finished, you may want to add some background — perhaps a few trees to suggest jungle. How about some grass in the foreground?

After you have completed this drawing of the elephant, try another one. See if you can find a better way of drawing him. You may want to work larger or smaller. Or you may want to change the pose — perhaps tilt the head or shift the feet. There is no reason whatever for sticking exactly to the photograph.

When you have drawn the elephant several times, try the lion. Work in the same way as when you were drawing the elephant. Look at the animal carefully. What impresses you as the lion's special quality? Is it his wild, fierce look? Is it his mane? The lion's mane is great fun to draw. Will you use little jagged lines, pretty curls, scratches, blots, scrawls, small circles? Whatever you decide to do, do it *consistently*, and the mane will have a definite texture.

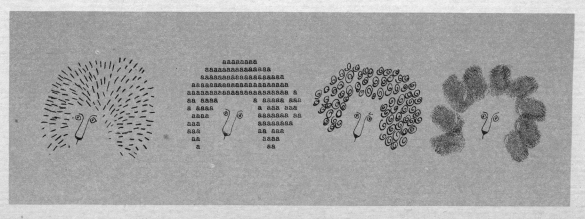

There is no one correct way to make a drawing. There are certain steps and methods of working, discussed in this book, that will help you to do what you want. But they are only techniques. It is your privilege and freedom to choose the sort of drawing you want to make. By all means draw a six-legged elephant with polka dots and feathers if the idea intrigues you.

The illustrations on these two pages show how different artists chose to draw a lion. The three drawings on the page opposite are based on the photograph of the lion reproduced on page 8. As you can see, each artist saw the lion very much in his own way!

JOE LASKER

MAURICE SENDAK

H. WEISS

13

MAURICE SENDAK

JACOPO DA PONTORMO

H. WEISS

14

Drawing the Figure

A thoughtful artist once said, "It's not enough to draw what a thing looks like. You have to draw what it *is* and what it is *doing*." This is particularly true when you draw the human figure.

One way to get the feeling, movement, and mood of a figure is to look for and recognize the *action lines*. Action lines reveal the position of the body and show what it is doing. Action lines don't usually appear as such. They are *imaginary* lines. Sometimes just one or two lines can show the action, as in the figures below. Sometimes three or four action lines are needed, as for the juggler.

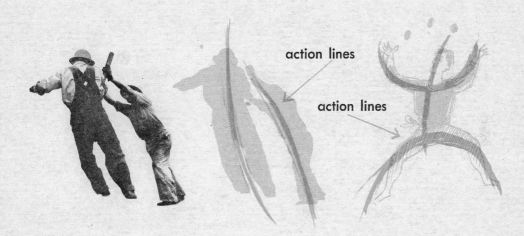

action lines

action lines

The fact that these lines are called *action lines* does not mean that they exist only in moving things. They exist in everything that has a shape or form. Sometimes it is hard to puzzle out what they are — especially if your subject is wearing a lot of bulky clothes or is all hunched up. But the action lines are always there. Look at some of the drawings on page 14. See if you can discover the action lines.

How to Draw the Figure

Of all the busy people on the page opposite, the tennis player has the simplest action lines. So let's start with him.

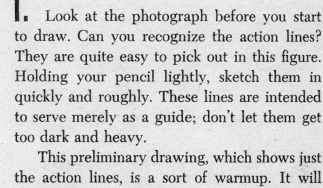

1. Look at the photograph before you start to draw. Can you recognize the action lines? They are quite easy to pick out in this figure. Holding your pencil lightly, sketch them in quickly and roughly. These lines are intended to serve merely as a guide; don't let them get too dark and heavy.

This preliminary drawing, which shows just the action lines, is a sort of warmup. It will help you to get started. It may look like a quick scribble or a tangle of lines. But if it has the feeling of running and reaching, you are off to a good beginning.

2. Now start to work on your main shapes. It is easiest to draw these shapes with the use of ovals, the way you drew the elephant. Each part of the body can be represented by an oval —a large oval for the chest, a smaller one for the hips, two long ones for each leg, and so on. The drawings below show how this works.

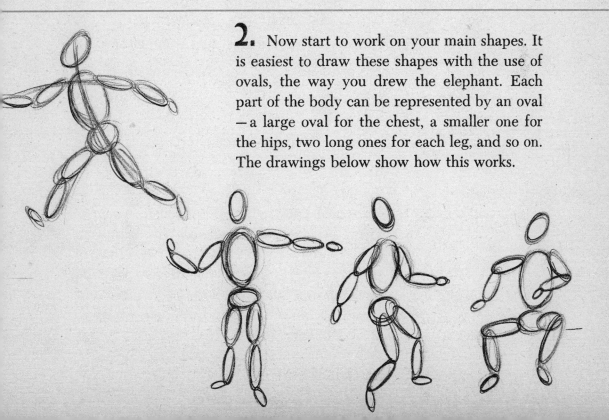

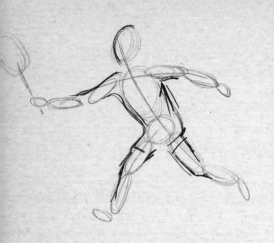

3. Action lines and ovals: when you have this much on paper, you have done the most important part of your drawing. Now you can begin to add your outlines. If the lines you put down at first are not exactly what you want, don't erase them. Ignore them and draw in other lines. Notice all the lines in the drawing on the page opposite. Too much erasing would give your drawing a fussed-over, sloppy look.

4. Skip from one part of the figure to another as your drawing progresses. This is the way to make all the different parts fit in with one another. With your action lines and ovals as a guide, you can be sure of getting everything in the right place. A common fault is to start at the top and work down. Often by the time you reach the feet, the top of the drawing looks like something started by someone else.

5. Once your outline is complete, you can give a little attention to detail. You may want to show some of the wrinkles in the shirt or pants. You may want to put in the socks and belt. But don't include all the little details just because you see them. Include only what you think will look well.

6. The next step is a criticizing one. Put down your pencil. Look at what you have done. Do you see anything you can improve — a line that needs strengthening, a curve that needs changing? Don't struggle too hard with your first drawing, however; start another and see if you can do better.

After you've made two or three sketches of the tennis player, you will probably want to draw something else. Try the wrestlers, or the women fencing. Either subject is exciting — filled with action and many interesting lines and shapes. There are two figures in each case, and their action lines are not quite as simple as the tennis player's. But if you work according to the method that you used for the tennis player — first action lines and then ovals — you won't have any trouble.

HONORÉ DAUMIER

Drawing from Life

To draw the figure well, you need much practice. You can learn a good deal by sketching from photographs, but it is hard to find clear and interesting ones. A real-life subject can be seen more clearly, and gives you a more vivid idea of feeling and pose.

Try to get friends or relatives to pose for you in different positions. Get into the habit of sketching the people around you, even if they don't hold still. You can make sketches at the beach, at ball games, looking out the window—wherever there are people.

JOE LASKER

MAURICE SENDAK

JOE LASKER

TINTORETTO

Pen and Ink

The drawings on the facing page were made with pen and ink. This way of working gives you very crisp, sharp lines and dense blacks (and you can't erase). Try some pen-and-ink drawings. Use an old-fashioned penholder and a medium-sized point. If possible, use the special artists' black ink called India ink and a smooth white bond paper (rough, absorbent paper might blot).

Although your final drawing will be in ink, make your action lines and ovals in pencil first. If they are too conspicuous in your finished ink drawing, you can erase them.

Drawing from Imagination

When you've had a little experience drawing people, you may want to make up some figures in various imaginary attitudes and actions. How would a trapeze artist look, and what would he be doing? What about drawing an acrobat, a football player, a ballet dancer, a colonel in the czar's cavalry? When you work from imagination, you must try to visualize the special qualities of your subject (just as you did with the animals described on page 7).

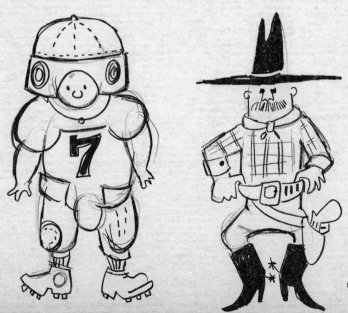

Fashion and costume designers draw figures all the time, though their emphasis is on clothing and not on what the people are doing. You can rough in a figure for this kind of drawing with simple ovals and then proceed to dress it! Perhaps you can invent some exotic costumes. What would you wear to a costume party or a masquerade ball? Would you dress as a jockey, a tramp, a deep-sea diver, a knight in armor? Enliven your finished drawings with a touch of color.

ROBERT ANDREW PARKER

H. WEISS

23

Tones

A *tone* is a shade of black or a shade of color. When you use a tone combined with simple line, your drawing will look more solid and more interesting. Here is a way to make a figure drawing, using tones. Get a small sponge, or a piece of sponge. (If you can't find a sponge, a crumpled-up facial tissue will do.) Pour two or three drops of ink onto a plate and add about two tablespoons of water. Mix the ink and water. Dip your sponge lightly into the mixture. Then press the sponge down lightly on a piece of scrap paper and quickly lift it straight up again. You'll see that the sponge leaves a large and pleasantly textured tone of gray.

Use the sponge to put the main masses of the figure on paper — a few big dabs for the body, some slimmer dabs (with the narrow part of the sponge) for the arms and legs. *Then* take your pencil, or pen and ink, and draw in the figure with lines. Try using colored ink, instead of black ink, for your tones. Or use water color, which is a transparent paint.

The drawing in the lower right-hand corner of the page opposite was made with white paint sponged onto colored paper.

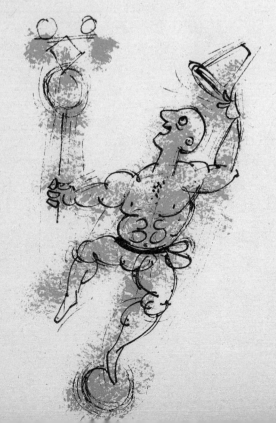

EDGAR DEGAS

ALPHONSE LEGROS

1526
VIVENTIS·POTVIT·DVRERIVS·ORA·PHILIPPI
MENTEM·NON·POTVIT·PINGERE·DOCTA
MANVS

ALBRECHT DÜRER

HENRI MATISSE

JOE LASKER   JOE LASKER

Drawing Heads

A person's face can tell you so much! It mirrors disappointment, surprise, pleasure. A face will tell you if a person is jolly or serious or sad. A face, then — a head — is always interesting to draw.

Each drawing on the page opposite has the special feeling of a particular person. The drawing in the upper left-hand corner of the page opposite, by Edgar Degas, captures the poise and grace of the ballet dancer he was sketching. The drawing by Matisse (lower right) shows the smooth, flowing lines and intricate patterns that the artist found most interesting.

Artists often draw portraits that look very much like the subject. The drawing by Albrecht Dürer (lower left) is probably an accurate portrait of somebody. (It was done in the sixteenth century, so you can't very well compare it with the subject.) However, in the heads you are about to draw, don't bother about a likeness. You can try portraits a little later on, after you've had some practice.

BEN SHAHN

Before you can recognize and draw the special quality of a head, you must know where the features normally go. One person's idea of the average, typical head is illustrated above. It is a drawing made in the sixteenth century by Leonardo da Vinci. The ruled lines show how he divided up the head into certain definite proportions.

You can make a similar "classic" head for yourself in the following way:

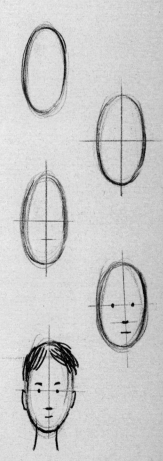

1. Draw an oval.

2. With light lines, divide the oval in half both horizontally and vertically.

3. Divide the lower half of the oval in half again.

4. Add a few dots and dashes, as illustrated, and you have a head with all its features in the typical position.

5. Put in a few lines for hair, ears, and neck, and you have finished your "classic" head.

That was easy. But for a drawing that has any feeling and character, you will have to do more than make an oval and a few dots and dashes.

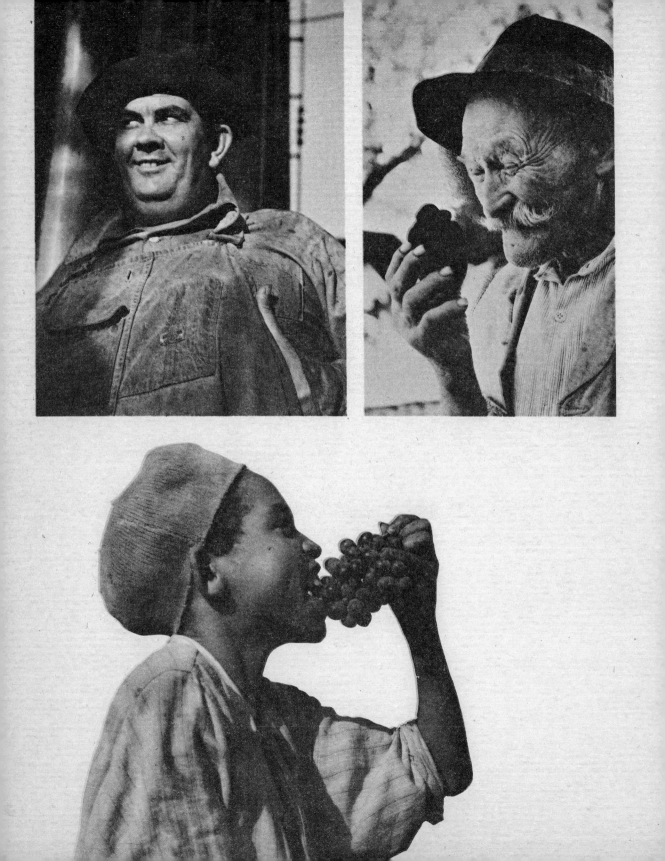

How to Draw a Head

Photographs of heads are reproduced on the page opposite to show you how various features look. For your first few drawings, try mainly to place all the features. Remember, a likeness is not important.

1. Let's start with the big fellow wearing a hat, in the top left-hand photograph. Look for the basic shape of his head. It is a simple, broad oval. Pencil it in lightly.

2. Now think about the features. The nose is a good starting point. It's a sort of landmark. This fellow has a big, pudgy nose that could certainly be drawn as a simple U-shaped line.

3. Next come the eyes. An eye is often drawn as an oval with a circle inside. But it can be done in any number of other ways. You can make a black smudge, a simple dot, a dash, or a circle.

4. As you work, think about the entire head, not just the part you are drawing at the moment. This will help you to fit all the parts together. The mouth has a lot to do with expression. If the corners of the mouth are turned down, you get a frown. If they are turned up, you get a smile. If you draw a circle, the mouth is open. You can draw our model's mouth with two wide arcs.

5. You can suggest the hat with three broad ovals, and the ears with simple loops. The chin and neck are round, fat curves. Most of the lines and shapes in this drawing are big and pudgy. This is the character of the man you are drawing, and this is the quality you want to get down on paper.

6. You can finish your drawing with the suggestion of shoulders and chest.

Take a careful look at what you have done, then put your drawing aside and try some of the other heads reproduced on page 30. Work as you did for the first drawing, looking for basic shapes and simple lines that will capture the character of your subject. If you do lots of heads, you'll find your work getting better and better.

When your drawings begin to look as if they might resemble actual people, you might try drawing someone you know. Get a friend or relative to pose for you.

There is one model who is always available. That is you! All you need is a good-sized mirror. Prop it up on your worktable, and you can draw yourself. Practically all artists have done self-portraits at one time or another. Rembrandt made dozens. He would paint his own picture whenever there was no one else available to pose for him.

PAUL CÉZANNE

How about making up some imaginary heads? How would a pirate look with a beard and moustache and a patch over one eye? How would a gangster look, or a beggar, or a man from Mars, or King Arthur? Can you make up a sad head, a silly head, a frightened head, a horrible head?

H. WEISS

VINCENT VAN GOGH

BERNARD KARFIOL

PAUL KLEE

Drawing Landscapes

If you tried to draw every leaf on a tree, or every grain of sand on a beach, your task would be impossible. You can't draw nature exactly as you see it. Nobody can. Only a camera copies precisely what it sees.

The artist's job is to make a picture that shows how he thinks and feels about his subject. He may try to tell in his drawing how it *feels* to be in a grassy meadow, or he may try to capture the wetness of a rainstorm, but he does not draw every single blade of grass or every drop of rain.

The drawing by Vincent van Gogh opposite is a good example of how an artist will change and simplify his subject matter to suit himself. No cypress tree ever looked like the one Van Gogh drew. But he evidently found the spiraling, flame-like foliage of the cypress very appealing, and this quality is apparent in every part of his drawing. Another artist might have reacted to the very same tree by drawing an altogether different picture.

A drawing is a personal expression in which the subject may be changed, rearranged, simplified, or turned topsy-turvy to suit the artist.

LEONARDO DA VINCI

MAURICE UTRILLO

How to Draw a Landscape

Look at the photograph reproduced above. Pretend you are sitting under a shady oak on a hilltop. Directly before you lies a peaceful valley, with trees and neighboring mountains, and you also see a little hilltop town. If you work from this photograph, you will be able to follow, step by step, a systematic way of doing a landscape drawing with wash.

Wash is ink (or black water-color paint) mixed with water. The more water you add to the black, the lighter the tones. Wash is a way of getting a rich variety of soft grays. Its name comes from the manner in which the tone is applied. It is "washed" onto the paper with a large soft water-color brush. It is usually brushed on very freely and loosely.

MATERIALS: You will need pen and ink (India ink is best), pencil, a large soft water-color brush, two or three small dishes in which to mix your washes, and paper. The paper should be quite heavy, so that it will not wrinkle when you put the wash on. Use a smooth water-color paper or Bristol board.

You approach a landscape in the same way as your other drawings. Look for the main shapes and forms. What interests you especially? Do you want to concentrate on the tree in the foreground, or on the little hilltop houses, or perhaps on the mountains in the background? Is there something you want to change or add or leave out?

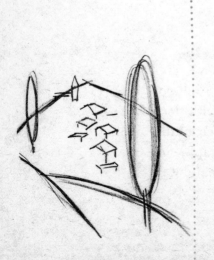

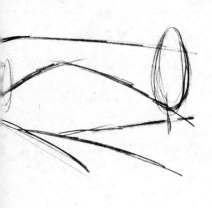

1. First pencil in the main forms very lightly. One main form is the mountains, another the hill with the town, another the large tree on the right, still another the road in the foreground. When you pencil in the main shapes, you are *composing* your picture. The way you combine the lines and shapes of your picture, and the way you arrange them on paper, is called *composition*. There are three drawings on the page opposite, all from the same photograph. Each is composed in a different way.

2. Now for the wash. Put two or three drops of ink on a plate. Or put some black water color on a plate. Then add three or four tablespoons of water and stir the mixture with your brush. If you want a lighter gray, use more water. Start with a light tone. You can always darken a light gray by adding more wash — later on in your drawing — but you can't make a dark tone any lighter once it has been brushed onto the paper.

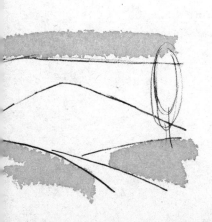

3. When you have mixed the wash, brush in a tone wherever you feel you need it — perhaps in the sky, or the mountains in the background, or the road or tree in the foreground. The area covered with wash will immediately become separate from the rest of your drawing.

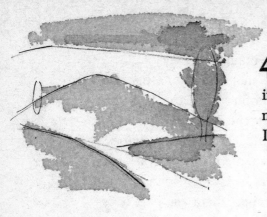

4. Give the wash a few minutes to dry. Then, if you think it should be darker, add some more wash. Don't draw lines with the wash. Do that later with your pen and ink.

5. Once all the tones are in, you can begin to draw with pen and ink. If you draw over a part of the paper that is wet, the ink will run. This can look pleasing; but when you don't want the ink to run, you must let the wash dry completely.

6. There are a great many small houses, trees, and shrubs in this landscape. Don't feel that you have to include everything. You can eliminate whatever seems too cluttered or unclear or unimportant.

7. Pen and ink are good for suggesting texture. There are many different textures in this landscape; use them to give your drawing some variety. The foreground and the foliage of the tree, for instance, would be enriched by a little texture.

8. When you finish the pen-and-ink part of the drawing, you may want to go back and add some more wash—perhaps a deep shadow here and there, or an accent, or a slightly darker tone somewhere.

JOE LASKER

LEONARDO DA VINCI

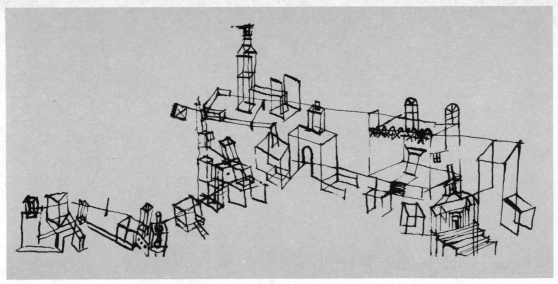

PAUL KLEE

Try another drawing from the same photograph. Compose your picture differently, and put your washes in different places. See what varying effects you can get. Try a drawing without the wash. You learn a great deal by drawing one subject several times and by doing it differently each time.

Now that you've tried a landscape, go out and sketch some of the neighboring countryside. Is there a park or a lake in your neighborhood? What about drawing a city landscape? Can you draw what you see from your window?

Try using color, instead of black, to make your wash. This will really brighten up a drawing. Make sure that you use *transparent* water color, and not a heavy tempera or poster color.

MAURICE SENDAK

Showing Space

How do you make a building look solid? When you draw the floor in a room, how do you make it look like a floor, and not a wall? How do you show that something is far away, or close? These questions are answered by the rules of perspective. *Perspective* is the technique of getting an object to look correctly in place when drawn on paper. There are five basic rules:

1. A basic principle of perspective is that things look large when close, and small when far away. For example, if you look at a row of telephone poles, you will see that they seem to get smaller as they get farther away.

2. Objects close to you usually appear darker and more vivid than objects in the distance. Have you ever stood on a hilltop (or looked out the window of a tall building) and noticed how houses or mountains far away seem hazy and vague, whereas a tree or roof close by is sharp and clear?

3. Objects close to you will overlap whatever happens to be behind them. For example, in the drawing on the left, the glass is farther away than the bottle. Therefore the bottle overlaps the glass.

4. Objects that are far away from you usually appear higher up than objects close to you. For example, a road gets higher and higher as it recedes into the distance. (It also gets smaller and smaller, as the first rule of perspective explains.)

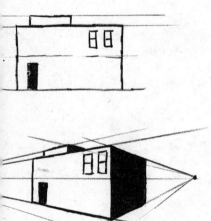

5. Parallel lines appear to come together far away, at the horizon. For example, the top and bottom lines of a building are actually parallel. This is apparent when you look at the building from directly in front. But when you see it from an angle, the lines seem to come closer together at the far end of the building. And if you extended these lines (or if the building were a hundred miles long), they would seem to come together at the horizon. Have you ever noticed how railroad tracks come closer together as they go toward the horizon? The same principle applies here.

Artists didn't know the principles of perspective until the time of the Italian Renaissance (about 1500). Drawings and paintings done before that time often tend to have a flat and somewhat strange, unreal look.

Today many artists intentionally ignore perspective. They feel they can best express feeling or mood and emotion by means of shapes and lines and colors. They would rather do this than make a realistic picture using the principles of perspective.

NUREMBERG CHRONICLES

WILLIAM GLACKENS

MAURICE SENDAK

REMBRANDT VAN RIJN

Drawing Scenes

So far we've discussed one-at-a-time subjects, such as animals, figures, heads, and landscapes. When a number of these subjects are combined, you have a scene. A scene usually contains one or more figures in some sort of setting, and there is usually some action. Sometimes scenes are called illustrations — they illustrate or describe an event.

Because scenes contain many different elements, they can become quite complicated. The scene by Rembrandt, at the top of this page, shows crowds of people, violent activity. But all of it hangs together well, and the final effect is one of great dramatic intensity. Can you see why some parts of the drawing are light, others dark?

How to Draw a Scene

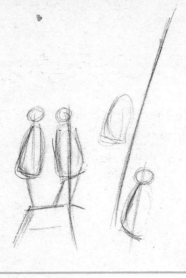

1. Here's a photograph of a scene that is filled with action and excitement. After you've studied it for a few moments, pencil in the main shapes very lightly. This is your "map," to show where everything belongs.

2. Now draw the two figures on the left, and the platform on which they are standing. (You can do this either in pencil or in pen and ink.) When you draw the figures, look for the action lines. Don't fuss with all the little folds and wrinkles in the raincoats.

3. Next, draw the fireman in the right foreground. In drawing this fellow, shift him a bit to the right so that he won't block from view the figures climbing the ladder. Artists often make this type of change to simplify a drawing. Most things are too complicated to draw exactly as they appear.

4. Now draw the ladder with the men climbing it. These figures are small and bulky, but you'll be able to draw them if you first puzzle out the action lines.

5. Now you are ready for some of the details — the railing, the hoses, the pipes, the rungs of the ladder. Don't clutter your drawing with everything you see in the photograph. You would do well to leave out some of that complicated bracing on the ladder.

6. A fire is exciting! Is there any way to make your drawing more exciting? How about smoke? There is plenty in the photograph, but it looks like fog or clouds. Draw some black, dangerous-looking smoke! How about flames? How about someone leaning way out of a window and crying loudly for help?

One way to make a drawing dramatic is to contrast light and dark areas with one another. Try this scene again, using wash and pen and ink. See if you can create a feeling of excitement by using the wash to make strong contrasts of light and dark.

There are other ways, besides wash, to get dark tones. Crosshatching with pen and ink is one good method. Crosshatching consists of many parallel lines drawn close together at different angles. The illustration below shows some of the many ways of getting dark tones with pen and ink.

EUGENE BERMAN

Draw this fire scene several times, but vary it each time. Shift some of the figures about, or add some more firemen and ladders, or change the size of your drawing. You'll learn a great deal by doing many different drawings of the very same scene.

Then you can look for other scenes. Picture ideas don't always come easily; you must form the habit of looking for them. Perhaps you will see something at home, or in the street, that provides good material for a picture. Have you been to the circus or the rodeo recently? Have you read a story or seen a television play that suggests a good picture? How about an imaginary scene — a train crash, the dramatic moment of a ballet, six men at work inside a submarine? Can you think of an interesting scene to draw?

PAUL KLEE

Experimenting with Pencil, Pen, and Brush

Life would be dull if you always did the same thing in the same way. This is true of drawing too. If you want to stay interested, and if you want to keep improving, you have to try different approaches and different materials and different ideas.

So far we have tried pencil, pen and ink, wash, and a few other drawing techniques. This section discusses some more ideas, some other ways of working with which you may want to experiment from time to time.

PAVEL TCHELITCHEW

HANS ARP

ALBERT ALCALAY

Lines, Shapes, and Abstract Drawings

This book has been concerned with animals, people, places — things that already exist. But an artist can make drawings that have no real subject at all — drawings that are simply combinations of lines, tones, textures, and shapes.

Suppose you wanted to draw a design. Perhaps you saw a flying bird and liked the lines formed by its wings. You might decide not to draw the rest of the bird, but just to make a design based on these lines. You could start your drawing with these lines and then continue, adding varied lines, shapes, tones, and textures as you saw fit, to get a lively, interesting design. You might try to capture the feeling of flying in your drawing. Your finished drawing could turn out to be quite elaborate without even resembling the original bird that you saw.

If you worked in this way, you would be making an *abstract drawing*. And this is just the sort of drawing that many modern artists find most interesting.

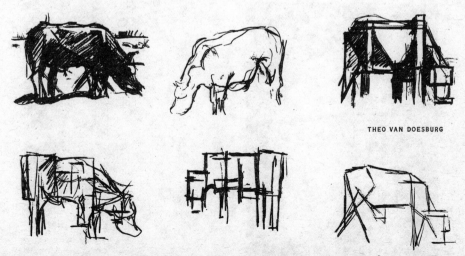

THEO VAN DOESBURG

Here are six drawings. They show how the artist experimented in an effort to find the most interesting lines and shapes in a cow. Some of the drawings are realistic, others quite abstract.

Exaggeration

Exaggeration is one way of making things dramatic. If you say that someone is as tall as a tree, you are exaggerating. No one is really that tall. You can use the same sort of overstatement in drawing to emphasize or dramatize an idea.

Suppose, for example, you make a drawing of someone who is always eavesdropping. You might draw ears as big as his head. No one's ears are that big. This would be exaggeration used to dramatize the idea that the person is an eavesdropper.

Or if, in drawing a head, you make your subject's pointy nose look like a needle, you are exaggerating in order to draw attention to this special-looking nose. Exaggerated drawings can be very funny. They are sometimes called caricatures. (The dividing line between a cartoon caricature and a fine artist's exaggeration is sometimes pretty thin.)

JOE LASKER

LEONARDO DA VINCI

Sometimes an artist will make extreme distortions in order to give the strongest possible impression of something. The mural "Guernica," by Pablo Picasso (reproduced below), is distorted and exaggerated in order to show most dramatically the ruins and horror of a bombed-out town. Guernica, a town in Spain, was completely destroyed by fascist bombers in 1937.

GEORGE GROSZ

PABLO PICASSO

Drawing Without Line

Most drawings in this book are done with simple line. The line is used to show the outline, or contour, of the shape you are drawing. But it is also possible to draw the area, or shape, without line.

In order to do this, you need something like the brush and wash, or the sponge described on page 24. Charcoal and Conté crayon are also good for roughing in large areas of tone.

Charcoal, which is burnt wood, can be bought at any art store. Conté (a nongreasy crayon) is also available there, and in several colors. These age-old materials were used by such artists as Michelangelo and Leonardo da Vinci. Get some special charcoal paper, which is best suited for charcoal and Conté. It has a slightly rough texture. A large sheet costs just a few cents, and it comes in many handsome colors.

If you take a small piece of charcoal or Conté and hold it on its side, you can quickly and in one motion make a large, flat, even tone. For a sharp line, use the tip of the charcoal or Conté.

line drawing

JOE LASKER

tone drawing

GEORGES-PIERRE SEURAT

charcoal

conté

You will find it interesting to use red or brown Conté crayon to rough in the big forms in a drawing. Then, if you want detail, go back over the drawing with pen and ink for outlines and accents. The rough colored crayon and the firm black line create a beautiful contrast.

After using charcoal, spray your finished drawing with fixative. Fixative — a thin, transparent lacquer or varnish available in art stores — is used to protect charcoal and pastel drawings so that they won't smudge.

GEORGES-PIERRE SEURAT

HERBERT MESIBOV

59

Spatter

Spatter is another interesting way of working. A spray of ink or paints is added to a drawing for the sake of tone or texture. The easiest way to spatter is to put a few drops of ink on the bristle tips of an old toothbrush. Hold the brush as illustrated below and draw your finger back toward you — away from the end of the toothbrush. As you do this, a fine spray or spatter of ink will be thrown off. With a little practice, you'll be able to direct the spray fairly accurately.

If you want the spatter to appear only in certain areas, "mask off" the section you want to protect. Use pieces of cardboard to cover the parts of the drawing you do not want to spatter.

Or, take a sheet of heavy paper and cut out of it the shapes that are supposed to receive a tone. Place this cut-out paper over your drawing to control the spatter.

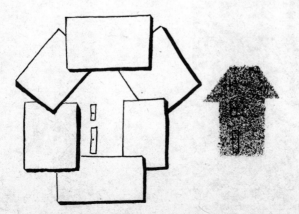

You can use spatter on a finished drawing, or you can use it as a background before you even start to draw. If you have some colored ink, try beginning a picture with spatter.

Toulouse-Lautrec was probably the first artist to make much use of this technique. One of the lithographs in which Toulouse-Lautrec used spatter is reproduced below.

Contrast

Contrast helps to make a drawing interesting. For example, a picture of a long, monotonous row of houses would be pretty dull if all the houses were exactly alike.

But if some of the houses were made dark and others light, there would be a contrast and the drawing would appear much more lively.

And if the houses had textures that contrasted with one another, the drawing would become still more interesting.

There are many other ways of getting contrast. You could make some of the houses larger than others. You could add color in some areas. You might also vary the quality of the line you use — light, heavy, jiggly, fuzzy. Or you might add a figure in the foreground or clouds in the sky. An artist often changes and shifts his subject about simply for the sake of giving his drawing contrast.

Anatomy

After you've drawn animals and people for a while, you may feel that your work would improve if you knew something about bones and muscles. Anatomy is the study of the parts of a body — how these parts fit together and how they work. Any number of excellent anatomy books have been designed specifically for the artist, and these will prove helpful.

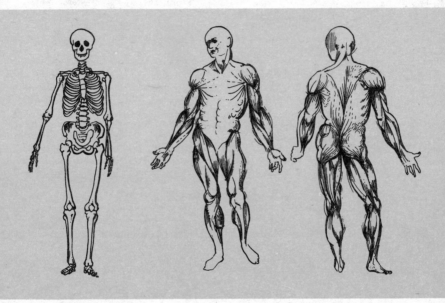

Other Books About Drawing

There is one book on drawing which this author believes should be on every artist's bookshelf. It is *The Natural Way to Draw*, a working plan for art study by Kimon Nicolaides, published by the Houghton Mifflin Company, Boston.

There are, of course, many books on special aspects of drawing, such as mechanical drawing, commercial illustration, pencil techniques, and so on. Such books are to be found in bookshops and in most libraries.

About the Illustrations

Some of the drawings in this book seem quite small because they have been reduced in size so that they fit on the page. In most cases, the original drawing is a good deal larger than the reproduction.

Where a page contains two or more illustrations, they are listed from left to right. The numbers below refer to pages.